With thanks to Jean Millar, numeracy consultant for
BEAM (Be A Mathematician), for her help during
the preparation of this book.

First published 2002 by Walker Books Ltd
87 Vauxhall Walk, London SE11 5HJ

2 4 6 8 10 9 7 5 3 1

This book has been typeset in Garamond Book Educational and Spanyol Bold

Printed in China

British Library Cataloguing in Publication Data:
a catalogue record for this book is available
from the British Library

ISBN 0-7445-8845-6

Carlo Likes Counting

Jessica Spanyol

WALKER BOOKS

AND SUBSIDIARIES

LONDON • BOSTON • SYDNEY

1 sun

Carlo and Mum
count one.

1 bird

1 sock

1 Crackers
the cat

2 bees

Carlo counts two
with his friend Nevil.

2 fleas

2 drinks

2 bananas

2 apples

2 caps

3 ribbons

Carlo counts three in the park.

3 squirrels

3 sticks

Carlo and Crackers count four.

4 leaves

4 sacks

4 pipes

Carlo counts five
in the café.

5 cups

5 hot-dogs

5 bottles

5 peas

6 baby birds

Carlo counts six over the stream.

6 spots

6 flowers

6 stones

Carlo and Dad count seven.

7
Bobbing Boats

Study with
7 Flowers

White Rabbits
No. 7

Still Life with
7 Oranges

7-House Town

Basket with 7 Kittens

7 red buckets

Carlo counts ten in the garden.

10 strawberries

10 tomatoes

10 seedlings

Carlo likes
counting
very much.

And he loves splashing!

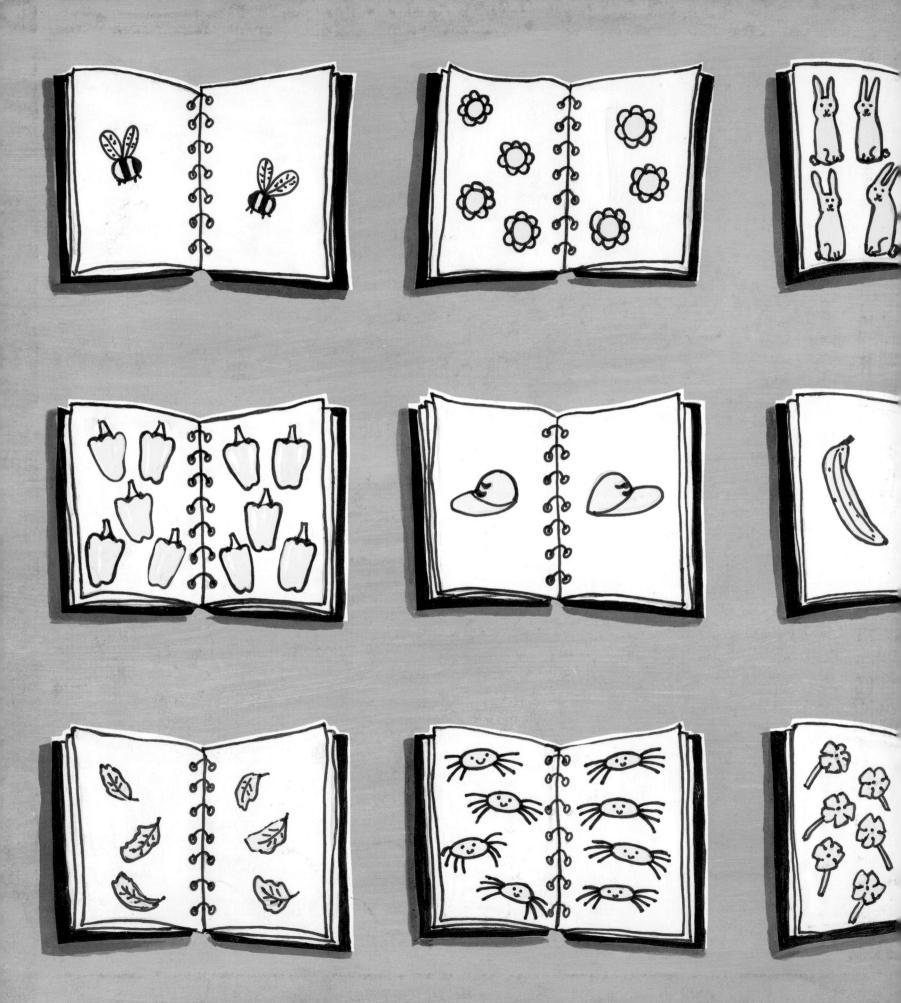